Pebble® Plus

Exploring the Galaxy

Pluto: A Dwarf Planet

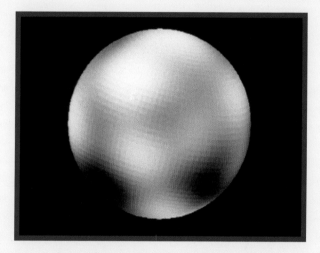

by Thomas K. Adamson

Consulting Editor: Gail Saunders-Smith, PhD

Consultant: James Gerard
Aerospace Education Specialist, NASA
Kennedy Space Center, Florida

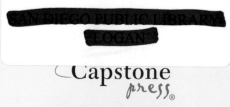

Capstone
press®

Mankato, Minnesota

Pebble Plus is published by Capstone Press
151 Good Counsel Drive, P.O. Box 669, Mankato, Minnesota 56002
www.capstonepress.com

1 2 3 4 5 6 12 11 10 09 08 07

Library of Congress Cataloging-in-Publication Data
Adamson, Thomas K., 1970–
     Pluto: a dwarf planet/by Thomas K. Adamson.
     p. cm.—(Pebble plus. Exploring the galaxy)
     Includes bibliographical references and index.
     ISBN-13: 978-1-4296-0736-0 (hardcover)
     ISBN-10: 1-4296-0736-X (hardcover)
     1. Pluto (Dwarf planet)—Juvenile literature. I. Title. II. Series.
QB701.A33 2008
523.48'2—dc22   2007003877

Summary: Simple text and photographs describe the dwarf planet Pluto.

Editorial Credits
Mari C. Schuh, editor; Kia Adams, designer; Alta Schaffer, photo researcher

Photo Credits
Corbis/Roger Ressmeyer, 19
Digital Vision, 5 (Venus)
Index Stock Imagery/RO-MA Stock, 15
NASA, cover, 1, 4 (Pluto), 7, 9 (Pluto), 19 (inset), 21; JPL, 5 (Jupiter); JPL/Caltech, 5 (Uranus)
PhotoDisc Inc., 4 (Neptune), 5 (Mars, Mercury, Earth, Sun, Saturn), 9 (Earth)
Photo Researchers Inc./Chris Butler, 11; NASA, 13; John R. Foster, 17

Note to Parents and Teachers

The Exploring the Galaxy set supports national science standards related to earth science. This book
describes and illustrates the dwarf planet Pluto. The photographs support early readers in understanding the text.
The repetition of words and phrases helps early readers learn new words. This book also introduces early
readers to subject-specific vocabulary words, which are defined in the Glossary section. Early readers may
need assistance to read some words and to use the Table of Contents, Glossary, Read More, Internet Sites,
and Index sections of the book.

Table of Contents

A Dwarf Planet

Pluto is a dwarf planet.

Dwarf planets are
round objects that move
around the Sun.

Dwarf planets are
too small to be planets.

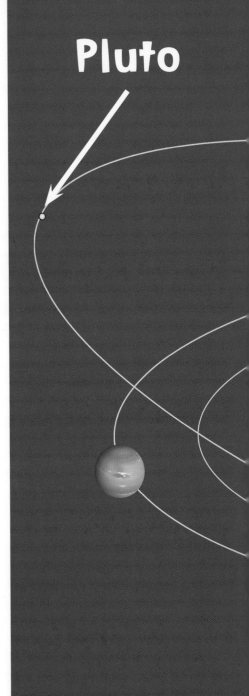

Pluto

The Solar System

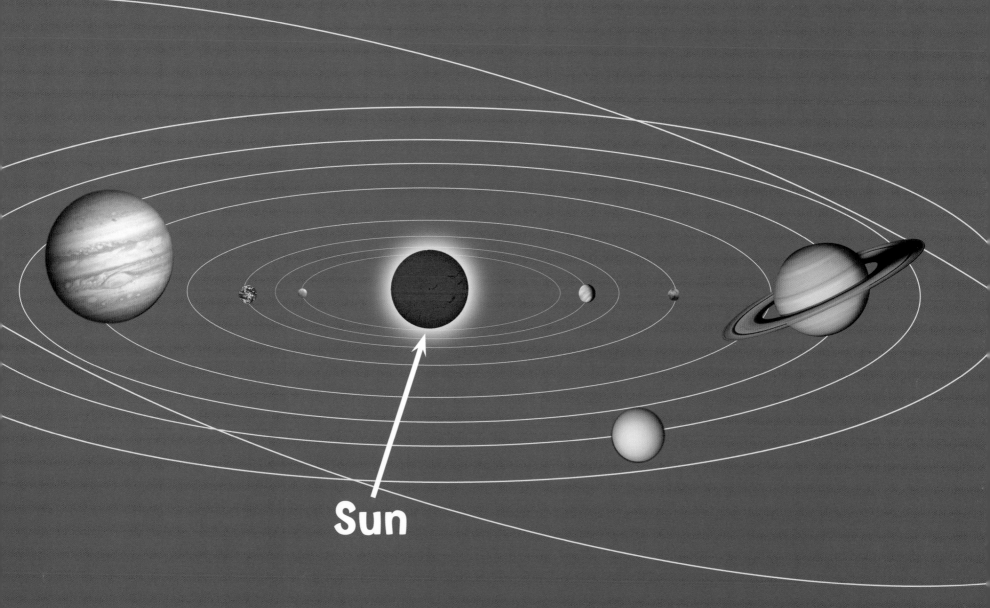

Sun

Pluto was once called a planet.

In 2006, scientists changed

the meaning of the word planet.

Pluto is now called

a dwarf planet.

Pluto's Size

Earth is about five times
as wide as Pluto.
Even Earth's moon
is larger than Pluto.

Earth

Pluto

Pluto's Moons

Pluto has at least

three moons.

Charon is Pluto's

largest moon.

Charon

Features

Scientists know only a little
about Pluto's surface.
They know that Pluto
is made of rock and ice.

13

Pluto might have some craters.

Craters are holes

shaped like bowls

on a planet or moon.

Pluto has a thin layer of air.

The air is usually frozen.

Pluto is very cold.

Charon

Pluto

People and Pluto

People cannot see Pluto

from Earth without a telescope.

Even through a strong

telescope, Pluto looks

like a fuzzy ball.

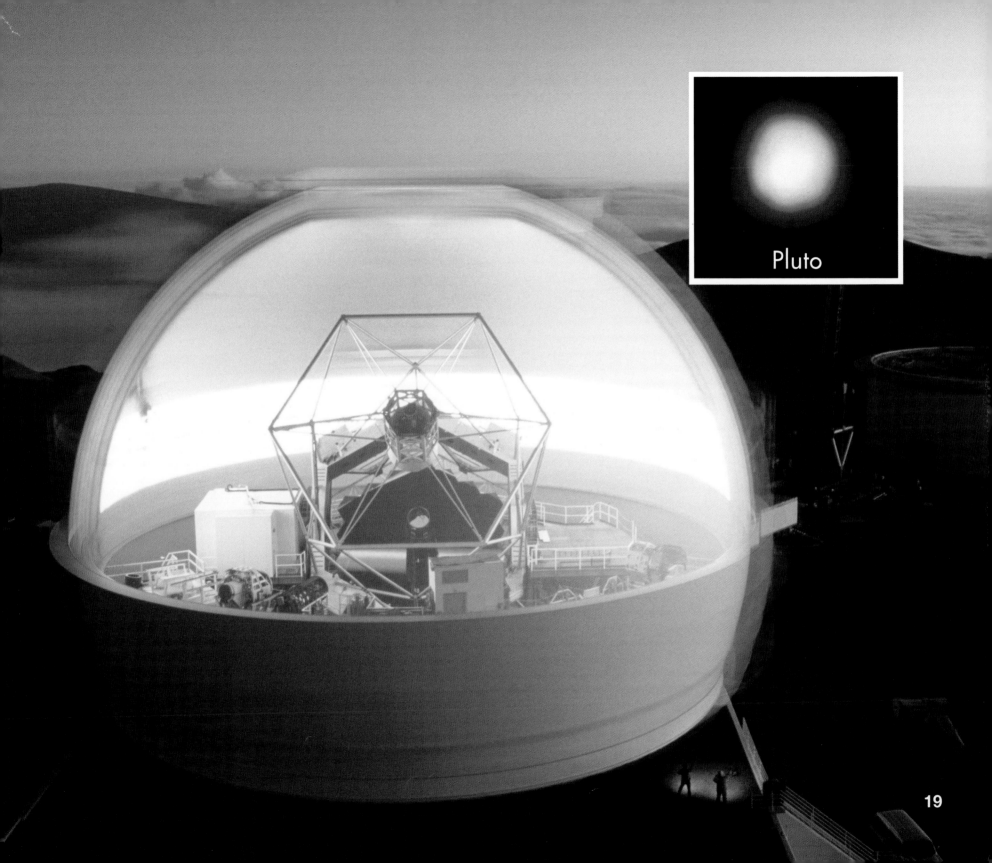

Pluto

A spacecraft is on its way

to explore Pluto.

It should arrive in 2015.

Painting of the *New Horizons* spacecraft

Glossary

crater—a large bowl-shaped hole in the ground

dwarf planet—a round object that moves around the Sun, but is too small to be a planet

Earth—the planet we live on

moon—an object that moves around a planet or a dwarf planet

planet—a large round object that moves around the Sun

scientist—a person who studies the world around us

spacecraft—a vehicle that travels in space

Sun—the star that the planets and dwarf planets move around; the Sun provides light and heat to the planets and dwarf planets.

surface—the outside or outermost area of something

telescope—a tool people use to look at objects in space; telescopes make objects in space look closer than they really are.

Read More

Bryner, Jenna. "Poor Pluto." *Science World,* 9 October 2006, page 5.

Kortenkamp, Steve. *Why Isn't Pluto a Planet?: A Book about Planets.* Why in the World? Mankato, Minn.: Capstone Press, 2007.

Orme, Helen, and David Orme. *Let's Explore Pluto and Beyond.* Space Launch! Milwaukee: Gareth Stevens, 2007.

Internet Sites

FactHound offers a safe, fun way to find Internet sites related to this book. All of the sites on FactHound have been researched by our staff.

Here's how:

1. Visit *www.facthound.com*

2. Choose your grade level.

3. Type in this book ID **142960736X** for age-appropriate sites. You may also browse subjects by clicking on letters, or by clicking on pictures and words.

4. Click on the **Fetch It** button.

FactHound will fetch the best sites for you!

Index

Word Count: 157
Grade: 1
Early-Intervention Level: 20